A Life In Darkness

The Drug
Addicted Child

by

William R. Jack

Bloomington, IN  Milton Keynes, UK

authorHOUSE®

AuthorHouse™
1663 Liberty Drive, Suite 200
Bloomington, IN 47403
www.authorhouse.com
Phone: 1-800-839-8640

AuthorHouse™ UK Ltd.
500 Avebury Boulevard
Central Milton Keynes, MK9 2BE
www.authorhouse.co.uk
Phone: 08001974150

First published by AuthorHouse 9/28/2006

ISBN: 1-4259-6523-7 (sc)

*Printed in the United States of America
Bloomington, Indiana*

This book is printed on acid-free paper.

Dedication

This book is dedicated to the memory of my son, to an amazing child, William Christopher Jack ("Chris").

Chris was a loyal, gentle, and loving child with the capacity to make people happy and laugh. He was for the earliest years of his life my constant and loyal friend, and never ceased to be, even in his devastating fight with drugs. He is terribly missed and deeply loved by his family, and we will always be amazed by the unpretentious nature of this child who taught us all so much about honesty, love, and detachment from the materialistic pursuits of this world.

Acknowledgements

I want to acknowledge first my son Chris for his constant loyalty and love, and the inspiration that he was to me during his short time on this earth.

I next want to acknowledge my wife Jane, without whose encouragement and support this book would not have been written and published. Her gentle persistence in this endeavor has been unwavering.

I also acknowledge my mother Ruth, and her husband Dan who were touched by the manuscript for the book and gave me further encouragement, and who were devoted to loving and helping Chris throughout his life.

I also want to acknowledge my brother Jim Jack who said this was a story that needed to be told, and further encouraged me to finish the book and have it published.

I want to thank my brother in law Bill Lawrence, and his son Peter for their leading role in Chris' memorial service, and the gentle and persistent love of my sister Jenny Lawrence for her tireless efforts, and her constant support during Chris' struggle with drugs, and her help in connection with Chris' memorial service.

I also want to acknowledge my two outstanding and loving children James and Nicole, who are still healing from the loss of their brother Chris, but have bravely moved on to fill their lives with love and joy in spite of their loss.

Contents

Foreword

Drug addition is a horrific illness that can have a devastating effect on the individual, parents, brothers and sisters, family, friends and on society as a whole.

This book describes one father's and his family's experience with the monumental roller coaster of a son's recoveries and lapses that can characterize this terrible disease.

It is hoped that this book will be of help to others who have to wrestle with this problem.

The death of a child is also one of the most painful experiences that any parent can be asked to endure in this life. It is hoped that this book will also be of help to those parents who have had to deal with the terrible pain of such a loss. The lesson learned by the author is that there is no one special way to recover from the death of a child. However, it is necessary to grieve in a healthy way for recovery to occur.

The names of certain institutions and medical practitioners have not been revealed because of the irrelevance of their names to this story. Turn Off Ranch was a real recovery center in Desert Hot Springs, California which has since gone out of business.

Bible Tabernacle of Canyon Country, California is still an active institution. It can be reached at 661 252 5087.

It is the author's opinion that drug addiction is a disease for which there is no cure and only three possible outcomes—insanity, death or a daily reprieve accompanied by continued life so long as the addict does not use. There is no cure for this disease in the author's opinion, only a daily reprieve from drug use during which time the addict can live a useful and fulfilling life. However, any attempt by the drug addict to use again will, in the author's opinion, result in a return to a vicious downward cycle of worse addiction and behavior that will result ultimately in his or her insanity or death.

The twelve step program of Narcotics Anonymous is recommended by the author as a possible route to the drug addict's recovery.

Chapter 1
Perspectives

On January 28, 1974 William Christopher Jack, Chris, entered this world. He was born at Scripps Hospital in La Jolla, California. His mother was Theresa Carol Asbury, Teri, and I, Bob, his father. In addition, Chris had a 12 year old brother, James and a 9 year old sister Niki. Chris was born much to my delight, but he was one of those totally accidental babies. We never expected to have him, he was just meant to be --clear and simple!

While our marriage of 12 years was going through a rocky period, for which I accept the lion's share of the blame, this child filled an empty place in the world and in our lives, and in countless ways would be a great blessing --as well as an incredible enigma.

While the state of our marriage was a major problem, I had no idea where it was headed.

For me, I did not want to go through a divorce, but life with Teri was getting more difficult all the time. She was unhappy, and so was I. Chris had come into the world at a very difficult time.

About this time I started looking in the area around Pasadena, near Los Angeles, California for a new job. I was seeking advancement, and even some separation from Teri, as our problems continued to increase. I also wanted to return to the area where I had grown up. We tried to keep these issues low key. Nobody, not even our parents, friends or James and Niki knew what we were going through. We tried to carry on with a normal façade.

I found a new job with a large engineering firm in Pasadena, California. This was about a hundred miles from our place in Del Mar, so I rented an apartment to live in during the week. It was very peaceful, but I wanted to be home on the weekends with my family.

This only lasted for a few weeks, then Teri got restless with the arrangement since she thought it gave everyone the appearance that we were separated. So even though she loved Del Mar, and was unhappy in the marriage, she pushed very hard to move to the Pasadena area. Chris was about two at this point.

During the week I was house hunting when I had time. Teri remained with Niki, Chris and James in Del Mar during the week, and would come stay at the apartment on the weekends and house hunt. The house in Del Mar finally sold, and Teri and the children moved in to the apartment. These were not easy or happy times, and when I finally decided on a very nice place in Glendora, where I grew up, she very reluctantly agreed and we bought the house in 1976. Strategically, from a marital stand point, this was a very big mistake on my part, since Teri did not like Glendora, but I did, and the housing market in Glendora was a lot better than in surrounding areas, it's a great bedroom community, which I thought would work to our long term advantage.

While there were some relatively good times in the next two years, Teri had pretty much made up her mind to leave the marriage, and in December 1978, under pressure to leave, I left the house and rented a place 20 miles away in Pasadena where I worked. The Glendora house was put on the market and sold without any difficulty. Chris was four years old at the time.

Our divorce was final in mid 1979. Chris was five, Niki was fifteen, and James 17.

What had at one time been a family was now a fragmented mess. Alcohol increased as a problem, and Teri and I, while we tried, had too much contempt for the other, and got caught up in selfish pursuits. Chris was in the middle of all of this. I was a weekend dad, and had no control of the family, and Teri showed no signs of wanting to control things in the house. Everyone went their own way, and Chris went from sitter to sitter during the weeks, and would be with me on weekends.

Chapter 2
Awakening

I remember the moment when it happened. Chris was about fourteen. I had been sending Teri and Chris to counseling at Teri's request, because the two of them had been arguing a lot. I was working at my job at the engineering company in Pasadena when I suddenly received a call from the counselor, Dr. Barney. There had never been any discussion of drug use by Chris. Teri had never mentioned it. Dr. Barney had never mentioned it. I certainly never detected any drug use by Chris during our regular visits. Little did I realize that the changes in his appearance, dress, the earring were all tale tale signs that something serious was going on inside Chris. I thought he was simply going through adolescent changes.

Suddenly, Dr. Barney is informing me on the phone that Chris' drug use had gone further than Dr. Barney had realized, and that Chris was asking to enter a rehab facility!

Dr. Barney suggested that his senior associate, Dr. Allan, an M.D., make arrangements to have Chris enter a drug rehabilitation center in Pasadena, near to where I worked.

I had recently taken a lease on a condo near the Glendora area where Chris lived. I felt the time would come when Teri and Chris would not be able to live together, and had moved closer so that Chris could live with me, and visit Teri on the weekends—a role reversal. But the news of Chris' extensive drug use, which had gone right over my head, took me by complete surprise.

Chapter 3
Nightmare of Drugs Begins

This was a completely new world for me—but things moved very fast. I picked Chris up that evening after work, and took him directly to the recovery center in Pasadena. The paperwork process went fast, forms to fill, insurance evidence and the rest. You think your child is going to be safe in one of these places. After all, they have the staff, and all the facilities. Chris was going to be here for 30 days. He was really into drugs deeply. They had a real grip on him. Much worse than I could have ever imagined or understood.

I visited Chris everyday. Sometimes twice a day. Teri would be there often, usually when there was an evening group session or she was done with work. There were one on one meetings, and group meetings involving parents, the young people and the lead counselors.

Some of these kids were there because their behavior was out of control, and there was some drug usage with them also. Then there were the more fragile, highly addicted kids like Chris. They were really in a high risk category, under evaluation, trying to give them tools to deal with their addiction to drugs. My observation was that the children with the out of control behavior problems were in a much more enviable place with regard to their prognosis. Chris was in very serious trouble in terms of his chances for recovery.

The participants in recovery, like Chris, were given one on one counseling, attended meetings (like 12 step program support group meetings), were asked to journal their feelings, and then meet in larger group meetings that involved their parents and other family members. Chris was also seen by his outside counselors, Dr Barney, and his associate Dr. Allan, M.D.

All the feedback that I got was that Chris had a good chance of slipping when he left the facility, so severe was his addiction. Therefore, I learned that we had a very sick boy on our hands, and that life was going to be very difficult. Just how difficult we had no idea.

One major decision that had to be made is where Chris was going to live—with Teri or me. On the day of Chris' release from the recovery facility, it was decided that Chris would live with me. Teri went along with this decision.

Chapter 4
Living With Drug Addiction

From the very beginning I tried to put structure into Chris' life. He had very little of that before. He was out of control. There was no way to know how Chris would respond to his stay at the recovery center.

There was the issue of school also. Chris was attending Glendora High School. He now lived in an adjoining City, Azusa, which was not in the Glendora High School District. This meant that I would have to try and get an inter-district transfer for him to attend Glendora HS. We were able to get both a release from Azusa, and an acceptance from the Principal at Glendora HS. The Principal was very understanding of our request, and was aware of Chris' situation. However, it was not long after Chris started that his attendance was poor, and the Principal called me in to say that while he appreciated the effort to keep Chris in Glendora HS that things were not working out, and he was forced to terminate the inter district transfer. Many days I would call attendance only to find out that Chris was not attending classes. I would make trips to the school to check on him. Chris denied the reports occasionally. Other times he had excuses for not being there.

So we enrolled him in Azusa HS where his attendance problems continued. One day he told me that on the way to school that several boys confronted him, and he had returned home. Basically, Chris had one main interest, and it was drugs, and he had dropped out of the system.

Then there were lingering legal problems because Chris had previously been involved with several other boys in a theft of sound equipment from the High School. We had to go to Court over that, and Chris was placed on probation. So now there was a probation officer to work with, and random drug testing. We were assigned a Judge in the Pomona Court system. Over the next few years we would visit him more than once.

On more than one occasion I would attempt to keep Chris out of the formal juvenile detention system for things he had done and would do. I thought he needed a family structure, and personal counseling for his drug and behavior problems, and that the juvenile system would destroy him. In retrospect I am not certain about that decision—I just wanted to give him a real chance to live like a normal human being.

After only a couple of weeks, Chris' drug and behavior problems continued. He had been seeing Dr. Barney, so with the support of Barney, Chris was taken back to the same recovery center in Pasadena for another 30 days. The depth of his drug use and addiction was very perplexing. It became apparent very early on that Chris was a child in crisis, and there were no ready made answers to how to go about getting things worked out.

Drugs were readily available wherever he went. His friends were almost all drug users, and they were present in abundance. These kids stick together, and are always ready to go for the drugs. Chris used many kinds of drugs—and he craved them all. He used pot to start with then progressed to acid and others.

Chris' second stay at the recovery center yielded a contract that the two of us had agreed to enter. We literally negotiated a list of his responsibilities, chores, curfews, and my responsibilities as well. We agreed to penalties up to and including confinement in recovery center for repeat drug use. We signed the agreement and both tried to make it work. But after a while Chris used drugs again, and he returned to recovery. This time to a new place in Rosemead, near Pasadena. Another 30 days. Then he returned home, and shortly after used again. Then back for his last 30 days at Rosemead.

A word on recovery centers, even the most "controlled environments".

Chris told me later on that his friends had freely brought him drugs at both the Pasadena, and Rosemead facilities. He was using drugs in the recovery centers. Drug addicts will get their drugs no matter what if they want them. Sex was also an issue in these co- ed places according to Chris. It is not out of the realm of possibility for a girl to enter one of these centers, and end up pregnant while living in "supervised " conditions". Drugs and sex are immutable and unstoppable in these places. Many parents get a sense of false security that their children are safe and free from harm's way when in "reputable" recovery centers. Nothing could be further from the truth.

In between recovery confinements, I had taken Chris on a trip to Yosemite, and Sequoia, then to visit friends in Northern California. We had a very fun time, and I kept my eye on him all of the time." Fragile" was the best way to describe Chris' sobriety, whenever he had it. The only time that I trusted him on his own on this trip was to be with the son of my friends. I was told later by my friends that Chris had smoked pot while he was with their son. One thing I learned was that "drug addiction" and "trust" were incompatible concepts.

Chris was plainly hooked. The only comparison that I had for Chris was my own father who had been addicted to alcohol as much as Chris was to drugs- --so I knew how intense these cravings could be—I had grown up with a father who also had them—only for alcohol instead of drugs. It had finally destroyed my father, and it was frightening to see these same cravings in Chris—I constantly feared for the worst.

During the second confinement at the Rosemead recovery center a CAT scan was performed on Chris's brain. It purportedly showed that a mild stroke had occurred. So with the help of my sister Judy (a nurse), I made an appointment with a neurologist in Pasadena—Dr. Matsuda. Dr. M reviewed the CAT scan and spent time with Chris. When I went in to see her, she was very alarmed with his condition, but said the brain would heal if he would stop taking drugs. That was, of course, the dilemma—would/could he stop taking drugs.

No doctor that I ever talked to during the time Chris was with me or afterwards has ever told me how someone could get Chris to stop taking drugs. He was possessed by a craving for them which was so strong as to defy any logic.

After his second confinement at the Rosemead facility, fourth confinement in all, the drug problem had become so grave that I was at my wits end. I had no idea what to do, or where to turn for help. So I turned to one of Chris' friends, Lisa, who was making good progress in her recovery. She really cared about Chris, and wanted what was best for him, as did all of us who cared about him. Lisa told me about a place called "Turn Off Ranch" near Palm Springs. One of her neighbors had gone there, and after being there for a year, went out into the real world and was doing fine. Turn-off meant "turn off to drugs". The place was supposed to have a good success rate with addiction, and only took those young people who were last resort, just before they went out on the street. Chris now fit that description.

I called Turn Off to see if they had room for Chris, and would take him in. They did have room, but said that I must take Chris out there for an interview. They told me that he would have to demonstrate a real commitment to sobriety. I told Chris, and he was sad about possibly having to leave, and I was sad too. I knew that even in the midst of all the insanity that we were experiencing that having him leave would create a great void in my life—I would miss him with a passion.

We pulled together some of his clothes, and personal items, and got in the car. We drove to Desert Hot Springs where Turn Off was located. Along the way he said "please don't do this Dad", and as I write this about 15 years later, it still gives me deep pain. But I wanted his life back, and was willing to do anything possible to get it back. If Turn Off Ranch was the answer then that's what we had to do!

When we arrived there it was nothing fancy. But it had a warm and homey feel about it. There were sober young people all around. The boys had their chores. The girls had theirs. We were welcomed by a woman, and two men. Chris had on his earring, and had a good head of hair.

We were taken to the living room, and the two men sat across from Chris. They were accepting of him and made him feel at home. They talked to him for awhile about his drug addiction, then asked him the key question---"do you want to stop taking drugs"—Chris looked at them for a moment and said "yes". The men told Chris he was going to get a haircut, and that his earring had to go. They told him they wanted him to know that they loved him without the earring.

Turn off accepted Chris.

We got his things out of the car, and took them in the house. Chris and I hugged each other and said goodbye. I felt hope, and sadness about leaving him. He would be there a long time, many months. I was also told that we could not see Chris for two months—the time it would take to sober him up, and get him acclimated to the new environment.

There was one detail that needed to be handled, and that was notifying the probation officer, and getting the Judge to approve Turn Off custody. The Judge had remanded Chris into my custody, now that was going to change. We were able to go back to Court and get the Judge to approve this move within a few weeks. Chris was 16, going on 17, when we went to Turn Off.

Chapter 5
Hope Springs Eternal

In this Chapter I will describe the Turn off Ranch experience. I have a picture in my office of Chris, Niki and I standing together at Turn off on one of the family days. We are all smiling and happy. Chris has been at Turn Off for some months and he is sober and alive. He has a fine grin on his face, and his arm is around Niki. Chris has a haircut, no earring, a fur lined jean jacket, white pants, and a white shirt. There is a grin from ear to ear on his face.

For the first two months Chris was at Turn Off we could not see him. Turn Off was operated as an isolated recovery center, and based on the twelve step program principles of Alcoholics Anonymous. While I could not see Chris in this period I stayed in touch with one of the staff members who was Chris' sponsor. Chris had a very difficult recovery experience during the initial sixty days he was there—he had to experience withdrawals, and these were extreme in his case.

Imagine, 120 days in treatment centers, and he was still full of drugs when he arrived at Turn Off. To any parent with a drug addicted child, regardless of his or her age, I say you have no idea of what you are dealing with in terms of the power of this disease unless you have been there yourself. This is a terrible illness, and will claim your child's life, unless by the grace of God, and some miracle your son or daughter can hit a bottom that is so painful that the craving for drugs can be surrendered to a Higher Power, and left there!

Sixty days finally passed, and the first family day arrived. We all visited our boy.

It was a happy day to see him clean and sober—a dream come true. And you learn to hang on these moments when things are good.

During the next six months we visited Chris every chance we got. One time Teri and I went into town with him, and we put our differences behind us, and enjoyed a fine afternoon with Chris.

There was no reason to expect that anything was going to happen. I was enjoying the fact that my son was in a recovery environment that was working for him. The kids from Turn Off were involved in community activities in the Palm Springs area. For example, they relocated all the furniture from the old Palm Springs Senior Center to the new one.

They parked cars at a fundraiser. Turn Off made sure that the kids were busy, and part of the community.

Then one day after Chris had been at Turn Off for about six months, he and another boy played some prank at Turn Off---a forbidden thing they had done by Turn Off's rules. Chris' sponsor called to say that Chris was in a very bad position at Turn Off and would probably have to leave. I talked to Chris, and he was down about things, but admitted to having done what he did, and said he was unpopular for having done this thing, and felt bad. I did not have an immediate plan for Chris. I was really disappointed that things had turned in this direction. I felt for Chris. I was not angry with him, just disappointed in the outcome of events.

Turn Off said they would give me a few days to try and work something out. But before I could do anything, Chris left Turn Off taking only a few belongings with him. Last seen he was trudging down a dirt road from Turn Off Ranch.

Chapter 6
Next Stop, Bible Tabernacle

My first priority was to find Chris. I had an idea that he might get in touch with one of his good friends—this kid was really a good kid too---CN who lived in Glendora.

The least of my worries right then was that Chris had violated the terms of his probation, and that we would probably be back in court soon. I was concerned about where he was, and what state of mind he was in, and his safety.

I called Chris' friend, CN, to tell him what had happened, and whether he knew where Chris might be. CN was being true to Chris' desire not to be disclosed, since Chris was probably scared. But CN told me enough to let me know that Chris was safe and sound.

I waited to hear from Chris, and in a couple of days, I got a call from Chris to have me come and get him at CN's house. I drove over and picked up Chris, and he was fine. I don't think he had used again, but I still do not know, and it's of no importance.

Chris could not stay in Glendora, and remain sober, so I had to find a place for him where there was structure, and the kind of supportive environment where Chris could continue his recovery. I knew that there was always the threat that the Judge would confine Chris in the juvenile detention system.

In my opinion (and it might have been the wrong call on my part), I felt Chris would have a better chance in a supportive environment where people showed some caring for him. Somehow, I came across the name of a place in Canyon Country, California, called Bible Tabernacle. This place catered to the homeless, was very structured, and was based on Christian worship. There were clear rules to be followed—the leader was named Milt. He had a rough background, but through his own recovery, and devotion to Christianity, had become a very firm but tender guy. Chris and I attended an interview, and Milt accepted Chris into their program, and wrote me a letter to that effect so I could give it to the Judge.

I explained things to the probation officer, and wrote an impassioned letter to the Judge.

When we went to court the Judge addressed Chris. He told Chris that the Judge had another letter from Chris' father requesting that Chris be allowed to live at "this Bible Tabernacle place", and that he was going to give Chris one more chance and grant approval. But if Chris strayed again the Judge was going to put Chris in a tough juvenile boot camp. I think this put the fear of God into Chris, because Chris lived out the next year until he was 18 at Bible Tabernacle, and was then released—he was now of legal age and wanted to leave.

While Chris was at Bible Tabernacle he earned his GED and got his high school degree.

Chapter 7
Tough Love, and Disappointment

After Chris was released from Bible Tabernacle, I worked with the probation officer to have Chis' juvenile records sealed, and to get his final release from custody of the court.

This was accomplished. I was attempting to allow him to begin with a fresh slate. Now his record was clear, and he was free.

Chris had no place to go, so he opted to come and live with me. Before long he was back into drugs, and hanging with a bad crowd. His addiction to drugs was stronger than his motivation to do something with his life. This is the nature of the illness that he had. I had numerous talks with Chris during the first few weeks that he was with me, and they had no effect on his behavior.

I finally came to the painful realization that tough love was the only solution. So I told Chris that unless he got enrolled in school or got some kind of job that he would have to leave. I gave him two more months to take some action, but every painful day passed and he did nothing but drugs, and hang out with his friends. I was determined that this was not going to continue in the house. So just before the two months were up I repeated over again that he was going to have to leave if the conditions were not met. Chris did nothing. Two days before the deadline I again informed him of the situation. He did nothing. Then the most painful thing, the day before the final day, I informed him his time was up and that he was going to have to leave the next day.

Chris then made arrangements to live with his friend CN—who finally kicked Chris out because of his behavior. He then went to live with Teri. This did not work out, and Chris ended up on the street.

One night late I received a call from Chris. He was in Arcadia , California, about a half hour from my place. He was hallucinating—claiming that people were chasing him, and he asked to come home. I told him if he would agree to go into a recovery program the next day that I would pick him up and bring him home. I then set up a three way call between Chris, Mickey B (the recovery house owner) and me, and we all agreed on the plan. I picked up Chris in Arcadia, made up his bed, and he took a shower, had something to eat and went to bed. The next day I drove Chris to Mickey B's house in Northridge, California. I paid Mickey for 30 days of recovery, and then left them to get acquainted.

The next day I visited Chris. He was in withdrawals. I talked to him for awhile, but he said he was feeling too bad to talk, so I left him for the time being.

Two days later I got a call saying Chris was missing from recovery, but that they had found him and brought him back. Within a few days he was gone again. He did not return.

Chapter 8
Last Chance at Recovery

Chris had become a full fledged street person. He would occasionally show up at my work. I was always glad to see him. We would always get together and have dinner, then he would ask me to leave him somewhere.

I was married to Kay in July 1995. That Christmas, Niki and James were over at our house, and we went to pick up Chris, and he joined us for Christmas dinner. He had just returned from a trip to Arizona, and had wanted to spend Christmas with us. Niki stopped along the way to buy some new clothes for Chris. It was good to be with him.

Later, after Chris had left the last recovery house at Mickey B's, he dropped out of sight. Then one day he showed up at my Mom's house in Solana Beach,

California. He was with his girl friend, and was driving a Hugo that was hissing and whistling. My Mom, (Granny Gittings to the kids) took in Chris and his girl friend, and agreed to work with them on their recovery if they were serious about it.

Granny Gittings is a devout Christian, with the faith of Job. Then the most amazing thing happened--both Chris and his girl friend got sober—mainly through a program at Calvary Chapel. Chris took driving lessons, got his license, and a Toyota truck. He got a job at a local grocery store. Things seemed to be going fine—and then Chris' girlfriend broke up with him, and he went into a tail spin—it was terrible setback. He immediately got back to drugs. He still wanted to be with Granny Gittings, but his behavior became bizarre. Once he ended up way down in Mexico, and Granny Gittings got him home through the US Consulate. Everyday he would get up and walk the highway, and pan handle. He was showing all the signs of schizophrenia. His behavior could become threatening and violent.

One day in late December 1996, Kay and I drove to Solana Beach to visit my Mom, husband Dan and

Chris. My Mom was becoming frightened with Chris' behavior. Chris had physically threatened Dan.

I sent Kay home with the car. Then I took a long walk with Chris, and we talked about things. I related to him that Mom and Dan were at their limits with him, and his behavior.

They just could not take anymore, and that he was going to have to leave. He initially objected, then agreed to leave. He went back to the house and packed his things. I walked him out to the sidewalk. He had a Amtrack train ticket to Los Angeles, and the train station was just down the street. I gave him some money.

As he walked away from me down the street he would walk a few steps, then turn and wave to me. I would wave back and smile. I stayed put until he was out of sight. Bitter sadness was the feeling inside. I loved him so much it hurt.

In a few minutes I would join him at the Amtrack station, and we would get on the same train, and sit together, and talk. He was drinking beer—lots of it. He couldn't get the drugs any more and had switched to beer. This would be our last ride together—my son and me. As I write this I am filled with overwhelming love for him—for all the craziness he was the brightness and love of my life.

Chapter 9
The Realization

It was a sunny morning in late July of 1997. I was roaming around the living room of the small condominium in Glendora, California that I had rented for nine months until the lessee of my permanent house moved out in April the next year.

My marriage of two years had just broken up. The disappointment of another failed marriage was painful. I was not in a good place emotionally.

I also was missing Chris, who I had not heard from for over six months. The last time I had seen him was the previous December at the Fullerton Amtrak train station. He was looking out the window of the Los Angeles bound Amtrak train that he and I had been riding from Solana Beach, near San Diego. We got off for a moment together—just long enough to give each other a big hug and say "goodbye." He then got back on the train. He had a big smile on his face as he looked through the window. He gave us a big thumbs up sign. And then he was gone.

Chris was traveling on to Los Angeles. My wife Kay had picked me up in Fullerton to take me home.

Suddenly the phone rang. On the other end was my daughter Niki who lives in Wyoming. Her words were direct. " Dad, Chris has been in an accident and he was killed" she said. She explained that it had happened in Bakersfield, California. He had been in an intersection late at night. A car returning home from the Bakersfield Country Club had hit and killed him.

The shock was immediate. All I could say was "Oh no." To make things worse, Chris had died over a month before and none of us had even known it. He had died a "John Doe" with no ID on his person. Niki told me she was going to fly in from Wyoming to help with arrangements.

He was a high risk individual, and I knew that, but the shock and grief of his sudden passing overwhelmed me. All of a sudden all the moments we had shared together, every place that we had ever been raced through my mind. It was not the same world without him. Something was missing that would never return. My son was dead.

Chapter 10
Immediate Aftermath

At the time of Chris' death I was working as a contract manager at a global engineering company in Pasadena, California where I had been for over 20 years. I was also attending night school at Claremont Graduate University in Claremont, California, working on a second Masters degree. My life was busy. And then there was the divorce with Kay to deal with and all the emotional upheaval.

The day after Niki called about Chris I went into work to finish up a contract my company was pursuing. Several people, including the client, were expecting the contract. To this day I do not know how I managed to go in and finish up that contract, but I did. Then, melt down. I was overwhelmed by grief. Every thought was focused on Chris' death, and the changed world that I lived in. Life would never be the same.

I took the next several days off work to gather myself, and get ready for the service.

My oldest son, James, was devastated. Chris was his little brother, and James had tried with everything he had to straighten his brother out. We all had. Nothing ever took hold.

During the days following his death, Niki was all over the place helping with everything

She was a pillar of strength and our cheerleader. Chris' Mother, Teri, was in so much grief that she was still in denial. Even after Chris' remains had been received by the funeral home in Glendora she believed it was not him. After she saw the indelible little mark on his hand she finally accepted that it was Chris.

Teri and I had a strained relationship for most of the years following our divorce in 1979. We had some differences of opinion over how to handle the arrangements for Chris, but I decided to back off and go along with her, and in retrospect the removal of any friction was the best thing that could have happened. I had wanted to bury Chris in the cemetery in Glendora.

Teri wanted his remains cremated and spread at sea, which we ended up doing.

The funeral director told us that a family member must be present to witness Chris actually enter the crematory. Niki and James volunteered to go, but I decided I wanted to be with him right to the end so I went too. This part was extremely painful, because just before entering the crematory there was a moment or two when we actually saw Chris to witness that it was him. I recall touching his hair very briefly, and then he disappeared inside. I felt weak. The grief of this moment is impossible to describe. I will not even try.

Chapter 11
The Service

We had an open service at the mortuary chapel in Glendora. The chapel was full of friends and family.

While we invited a youth minister from Calvary Chapel who had worked with Chris in one of his attempts at recovery, the main service was led by my brother- in- law, Bill Lawrence, and we were blessed by the music and song of my nephew Peter Lawrence, Bill's and my sister Jenny's youngest son.

There was a large picture of Chris at the front of the Chapel right next to the flowers. It was one of those real great pictures of him with that warm smile of his at a time when he was sober and bright.

There were a number of parents and young people at the service. We wanted to be very open and direct about how we lost Chris and about his battle with drugs. We felt this was valuable testimony to every one of the devastating results of drug use.

We encouraged everyone who had something to say to get up and share their stories about Chris, and what they remembered. A number of his friends and others shared their feelings and stories about Chris.

The service ended with a bagpiper marching through the Chapel playing Amazing Grace. The place was filled with the sound of bagpipes --a tribute to our deep love for Chris. I am sure he was there in his spirit enjoying the music and knowing how much he was loved and missed, but knowing Chris he would rather have been there in person, and was not in the least bit happy with his fatal accident.

Chapter 12
Ashes at Sea

The day after the service the immediate family traveled to Newport Beach for the spreading of Chris' ashes at sea.

I could not accept that the only thing left of my son were those ashes. Something prevented me from accepting that there was not more of my son in this world. Any parent who has lost their child knows this feeling. No more smiles, no more hugs, no more voice to hear or laughter. It just wasn't right.

The emptiness was overwhelming. With time, these feelings heal, but at first the grief is just powerfully overwhelming.

We boarded the chartered ship, and started out through the harbor, then into the open ocean headed for a place that I did not know and cannot remember—although the coordinates where Chris' ashes were spread were given over to the family by the ship's Captain.

When we arrived at the place, the ship turned down its motors, and we all joined hands and said a prayer. Teri, his Mom, spread the ashes. And I could tell that this was comforting to her. The ship then returned home.

Chapter 13
Healing

It is healthy to grieve. I allowed myself to feel the pain. The more I allowed myself to feel the pain the faster I knew that I would begin to heal.

I am writing this almost nine years after Chris' death. Because of this I know that time heals. For those who have a newly lost child, it is impossible to look beyond the immediate overwhelming sense of loss, and see that there is hope beyond, but there is.

I was fortunate to have some tools at my disposal when Chris died. I had been the member of a twelve step program for about four years at the time Chris died.

This program had helped me to open up with others and talk about things before they got bottled up inside.

Also, during several of Chris' recovery programs there were opportunities to talk openly with individual counselors, and groups comprised of parents and recovering young people. These sessions helped me at the time to develop the tools to open up and talk about my feelings.

I knew that I had to make at least one visit to the place in Bakersfield where Chris had been killed. I ended up making about three trips. I needed to get closure on several issues. When I arrived at the place, I parked my car and went into a restaurant at the intersection where the car had struck Chris. I had pictures of Chris with me. I first spoke with one of the waitresses. She was not on duty at the time Chris had been killed but had heard about the accident.

There was an ARCO station on one corner, a Chevron station on another corner, a Jack in the Box on one corner, and a closed gas station on the final corner. I next spoke with the attendant at the ARCO station. He recalled Chris being there for 2-3days, and said that Chris was not careful about following the traffic lights. This person said he has spoken to Chris about being more careful when crossing the street. He also said that there seemed to be something wrong with Chris, in his behavior. That did not surprise me. This person said that Chris had been at the Jack in the Box immediately before the accident, and while this person had not seen the accident he showed me where Chris had been hit in the intersection, according to reports he had heard.

I next visited the Jack in the Box. One of the persons working there called the manager to come and talk with me. I introduced myself to him, a young guy in his twenties. He told me that he was on duty when the accident had occurred, and that it had been in fact he who had chased Chris off the Jack in the Box property. According to him, Chris had been standing at the drive through window asking customers for money, and this young man chased Chris off the premises. Chris had been drinking a cup of coffee, the last thing he had to drink. The manager said that almost immediately after he had returned inside the accident occurred. He said that his co-workers had chided him that if he had left Chris alone then he would still be alive. I told the young man that he was just doing his job, and that the accident would have just happened on another corner on another day if not that night. He told me that the ambulance had gotten there pretty quick, and that Chris was very still and did not seem to be in any pain. That had been a major concern I had –that he may have suffered and not been picked up right away. Next, I traced Chris' final steps, feeling a great deal of pain as I did so, but all being part of getting closure.

I then located the emergency room where they had taken Chris. I introduced myself, and asked if I could speak with the doctor on duty that night, hoping he would be there. Actually, after the hospital did a record search, it was determined that two doctors had treated him, and they were both on duty at the time. So they ushered me to a room and both of these doctors spent all the time that was needed to explain the seriousness of Chris' accident. His spinal cord had been severed in the area of the neck, and while he was still technically alive when he got to the hospital, he was functionally gone. He had no feelings, therefore, no pain, and the doctors said this was instant on impact. He died in the hospital. That gave me closure, and I will always appreciate those two doctors.

I made two additional stops. One at the County Morgue to see if there were any belongings, and to get a copy of the autopsy report. The report showed that there were no drugs in his system, but there was alcohol. But no drugs! The last stop was at the California Highway Patrol Office. I introduced myself, and asked if anyone could retrieve the file, and if I could get a copy of the police report. They got me a copy of the report, and showed me the file. The desk officer said although it was CHP policy to take pictures, that none had been taken. When I asked him why, he said "I don't know. What was your son doing in Bakersfield". They knew he was a street person, so they really were not that concerned. It left a sour taste in my mouth, especially after those doctors had been understanding. I left with the police report.

There were witnesses listed in the police report. They lived in Utah. I called them, and they indicated that Chris had been crossing the street diagonally, and the smell of alcohol was strong around him.

As far as the woman who was driving the car that hit Chris, I did not talk with her, although she probably went through her own hell hitting and killing Chris. If I could see her today, I would tell her something like I told the manager at the Jack in the Box---"it would have happened at another corner on another day."

Something else that was of immense help, and that continued for several years, was attending support groups made up of other parents whose children had died. I learned a great amount from these meetings, and the process was very healing to me.

One thing I learned was gratitude. There were parents who had lost their only child. I still had two left, plus grandchildren. While nothing could replace Chris, I slowly came to see that my loss, while immense, was not as great as that of some others. So rather than focusing entirely on my loss, I slowly started to attend these parent support groups to give a helping hand to parents who had experienced the very recent death of their child.

I still needed very much to open up and talk about Chris to continue my personal healing, but the emphasis slowly shifted from my loss to the losses of others.

Other things that I learned from these sessions were:

1. That everyone grieves differently. There are no rules. Anything goes. Sometimes a child's room is left completely alone. Nothing is removed or changed. Sometimes this is not the case.

To support the idea that there is no single way to grieve and survive the death of a child, my good friends Mary and Jim lost their son Marc in an automobile accident at about the same time as Chris' death. Mary and Jim found their healing in each other. They hung chimes on the porch, and when the chimes ring it is Marc. Mary says that the chimes ring sometimes even when there is no wind. So healing and comfort come in multiple ways.

2. There are no time limits to anything when it comes to the grieving process.

3. Husbands and wives grieve differently. Each needs to respect the grieving process of the other. A wife may want to attend a support group, while her husband seeks solitude. Both are healing in their own way.

4. The death of an unborn child, or a newly born child, or even an adult child, is as painful as the loss of a ten year old or a teen. It is the loss of the expectation of the life or the relationship that is grieved. The age of the child makes no difference.

5. Dates are important. The birthday of the child, the anniversary date of the death, holidays are all special dates or times. On Chris' birthday I place flowers at the cemetery where I put an engraved marker in his honor. I fly a helium filled balloon that says "Happy Birthday", and sing happy birthday to him. On his anniversary date for a number of years I had dinner with my son James and his family. My daughter-in law, Nery, burned a candle for Chris during the evening. Everyone will find their own way to recognize their child's special dates. There are no rules here either—no rights and wrongs.

6. It seemed to me that where a mother and father attended group sessions together that the two may have healed better, than where they went their separate ways in the grieving process. This is only my perception, but is worth noting.

7. Parents experiencing the death of a child frequently seemed to feel abandoned by long held friends. Another observation was the anger that these parents felt when a friend who had not experienced the death of a child would say "I know how much pain you must feel." Most

parents would much prefer to hear a friend who has not lost a child say something like "I cannot even imagine what you must be going through." This is worth mentioning because it is a frequent mistake that many people make when they are talking with a parent who has experienced the death of their child.

8. Parents who have lost their child always seemed to feel that there was something that the parent could have done to prevent it. This is a mind trap that all parents must learn to get over.

Chapter 14
Feelings and Physical Stress

I noticed for months that I was edgy and under significant emotional and physical stress. For example, I tightly gripped the steering wheel constantly. I was edgy at bedtime and could not sleep. On more than one occasion I drove from the Los Angeles area to Las Vegas late at night, only to return home the next day.

There were wild fluctuations in my emotions. Suddenly the realization of Chris' death would haunt me. I would become extremely emotional, sometimes moaning with grief, and breaking out into tears. At other times I seemed to be fairly normal. These fluctuations continued for months, becoming less severe with time. I never remember trying to resist these emotions, favoring instead to allow myself the full extent of mourning.

At first I had an insatiable desire to talk in group sessions about my feelings regarding Chris, and the sadness I was feeling. With time the intensity of these feelings lessened.

Today, nine years later, my feelings regarding his death are very manageable. I can talk about his death to other people in a quiet and straight forward manner. I mention this only because the parent who is new to the death of their child needs to know that if they grieve in a healthy manner now, that they will heal from this incredibly immense loss. There is hope up ahead. Life can be bearable and even joyful again.

About the Author

The author is William R.(Bob) Jack.

Bob is a native Californian, born January 4, 1941 in Santa Monica, California.

Bob is married and presently lives in North Las Vegas, Nevada with his wife Jane.

He has two surviving children by his first marriage. James, who lives in Southern California with his wife Nery, and two children Chris and Niki and his daughter, also Niki who lives in Wyoming with her husband Dave, and two children, Zach and Rick .

His youngest son Christopher about whom this book is written passed away on June 6, 1997 at the age of 23.

Bob grew up in Southern California in the San Gabriel Valley area not far from Los Angeles.

He graduated from Citrus High School, and Citrus College and received his BA Degree in Economics from California State University at Los Angeles. He later went on to earn an MBA Degree from Azusa Pacific University and a Master of Science Degree in Advanced Management from Claremont Graduate University's Drucker School.

Bob's career spanned 40 years in the aerospace, petroleum, academic research, nuclear energy and engineering fields. He spent the last 24 years of his career at a global engineering and construction company in Pasadena, California.

He is presently a member of the Board of the Henderson, Nevada Civitan organization which primarily assists the mentally and physically challenged.